VOCABULARY BUILDER CURSIVE HANDWRITING

Study Definitions • Learn New Words • Writing Practice Workbook

---

The Write-N-Learn Series

Douglas Grey

Vocabulary Builder Cursive Handwriting
Study Definitions • Learn New Words • Writing Practice Workbook
Copyright © 2018
The Write-N-Learn Series
Douglas Grey

All rights reserved. No portion of this book may be copied, reproduced, stored or transmitted by any means (including, but not restricted to, electronic, photocopying, recording) without the express written consent of the author, Douglas Grey. However, educators and parents who purchase this book may reproduce selected activity pages for non-commercial classroom or personal instruction.

ISBN-13: 978-1-941691-31-1

LEARNING TIPS

Writing aids with memorization.

In fact, you can learn four ways:

- First, read the word, definition, and example.
- Next, trace over the words written in cursive handwriting.
- Now rewrite each word on the blank line below.
- Finally, speak the word and definition out loud.

This way, reading, writing, speaking, and listening all work together to aid in learning.

UPPERCASE CURSIVE ALPHABET

A B C D E F

G H I J K L

M N O P Q R

S T U V W X

Y Z

LOWERCASE CURSIVE ALPHABET

a b c d e f

g h i j k l

m n o p q r

s t u v w x

y z

Abrogate

Abolish, repeal, or cancel formally (using authority).

The two companies abrogated their previous agreement in order to make better use of new technology.

Acumen

The ability to recognize new developments and to make good decisions swiftly.

Her business acumen helped her get promoted to division manager within two years.

Adulation

Admiration or high praise.

The adulation of his teacher and parents helped motivate the student to work even harder.

Aesthetic

Pertaining to beauty (or to the appreciation of beauty).

The visitors were given great aesthetic pleasure when the artist unveiled his latest masterpiece.

Alacrity

Eager willingness and readiness.

When she was invited to read her book at the local elementary school, the author accepted the invitation with alacrity.

Anachronism

Something that appears not to be in its proper historical period (often outdated).

It was an anachronism when the actor's cell phone rang during a play about ancient Rome.

Assiduous

Hard-working with attention to detail.

The students were assiduous in their research and planning of the assigned project.

Benevolent

Kindhearted, compassionate, caring, humanitarian.

The charitable organization appreciated the gift from the benevolent donor.

Brusque

Abrupt, unfriendly, or dismissive in manner or speech.

His brusque manner left her wondering if she should cancel their dinner date.

Calumny

A false, malicious, slanderous statement made to harm a person's reputation.

The politician refused to spread a calumny about his rival.

Camaraderie

Loyalty and friendship among a group of people.

The sports analysts attributed the team's win partly due to their great camaraderie among teammates.

Censure

Express strong disapproval (often in a formal statement).

Public censure of the corrupt politician didn't satisfy the people. They wanted him to be punished for his misconduct.

Circuitous

Indirect or roundabout.

They missed the opening of the play because the driver took a circuitous route.

Collaborate

Work together.

Students with much different skill sets often complement each other well when they collaborate on a research project together.

Condescending

Having a superiority or patronizing attitude.

His condescending tone left his peers feeling that he wouldn't be a good team player.

Conundrum

Puzzling problem or dilemma.

Working for two bosses proved to be quite a conundrum. It was often challenging to please both bosses at the same time.

Cursory

Done quickly without paying much attention to detail.

The students were frustrated that their teacher merely gave their science projects a cursory glance before assigning their grades.

Deleterious

Harmful (often to living things).

Smoking can be deleterious to your health.

Vocabulary Builder Cursive Handwriting

Demagogue

A leader who attempts to influence people through emotional appeals.

The rebellion was led by a gifted demagogue.

Writing Practice Workbook

Deprecate

Belittle or express disapproval.

Sports are much more fun when the coaches don't deprecate their players throughout the game.

Desecrate

Violate the sacredness.

Vandals desecrated the sacred monument.

Desiccated

Dehydrated or dried out.

The ground appeared desiccated after years of a drought.

Diaphanous

Light, sheer, and translucent (typically referring to a fabric).

Although the gown was beautiful, she decided not to buy it when she realized that the material was diaphanous.

Digression

Straying from the subject while talking or writing.

The teacher made a slow digression from lecturing about the cause of air pollution to talking about life on Mars.

Dither

Nervous excitement or confusion.

My mom was in a dither trying to get ready for the party to welcome my dad's new boss.

Divergent

Deviating from a particular direction.

Financial experts held divergent opinions regarding the best strategy for improving the nation's economy.

Ebullient

Very cheerful, enthusiastic, full of energy.

She felt ebullient on the morning of her wedding.

Egregious

Standing out in a bad way.

He was sent to the principal's office for his egregious behavior in the library.

Enervate

Make somebody feel tired and weak.

After a weekend of tedious chores, he felt thoroughly enervated.

Ephemeral

Short-lived.

Most fads are ephemeral.

Eschew

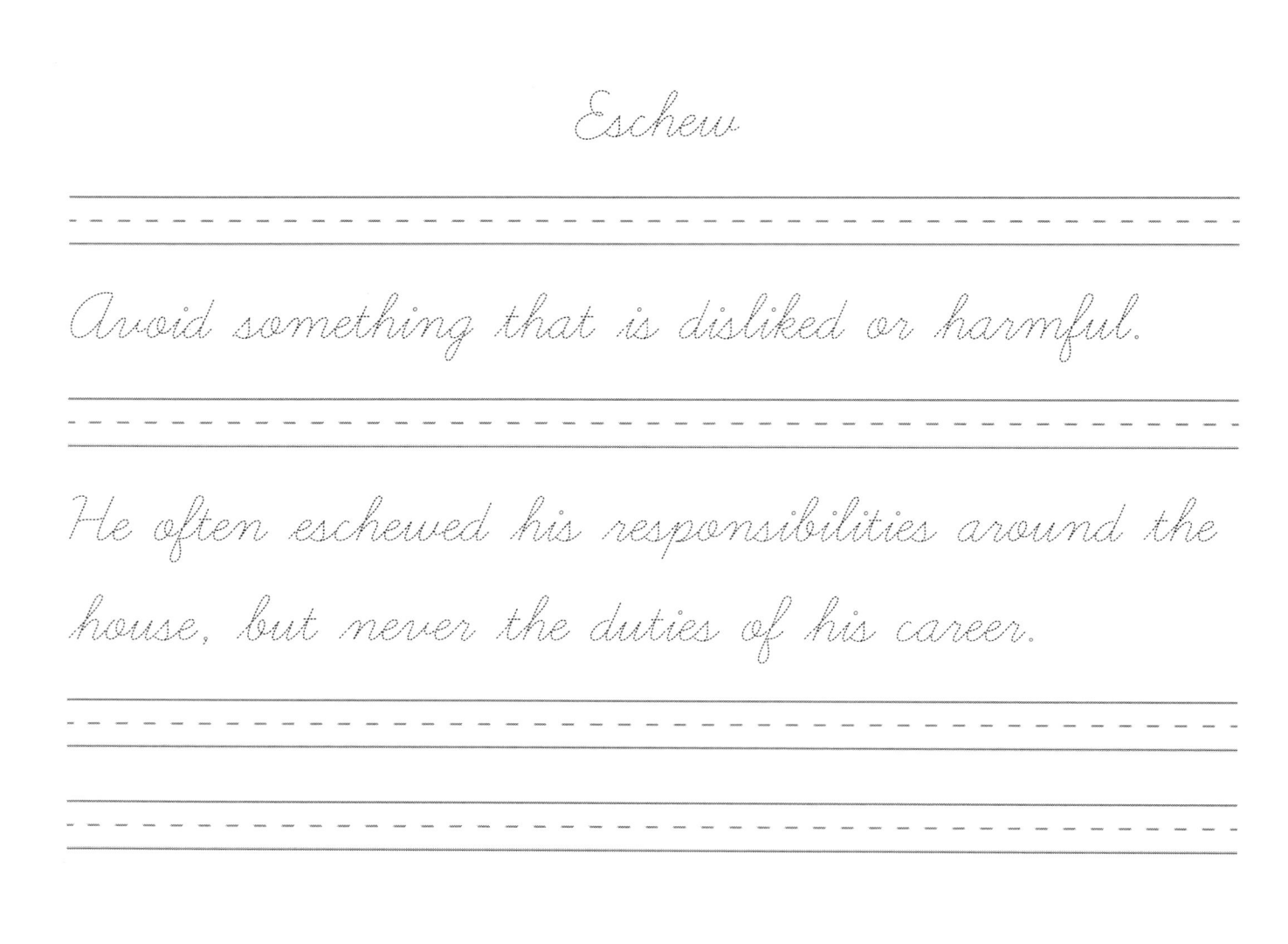

Avoid something that is disliked or harmful.

He often eschewed his responsibilities around the house, but never the duties of his career.

Exculpate

Prove that somebody isn't guilty.

The private investigator discovered evidence that would exculpate the defendant.

Exemplary

Serving as an excellent example for others to follow.

The exemplary employee always completed his assignments thoroughly and on time.

Exigent

Urgent and needing immediate attention.

In exigent circumstances, a doctor may perform surgery without getting prior authorization from the insurance company.

Expiate

Make amends for some wrongdoing or guilt.

His material gifts did not completely expiate his feelings of guilt.

Extenuating

Making a wrongdoing seem less serious.

Due to extenuating circumstances, the jury only found him guilty of the lesser charge.

Fallacious

Erroneous (often in a misleading or deceptive way) or based on an erroneous belief.

She was unfairly punished because the administration believed a fallacious argument.

Fatuous

Foolish, silly, pointless.

The professor was frustrated that many of his pupils spent hours engaging in fatuous nonsense and little time pursuing their studies.

Fortuitous

Lucky; happen by chance or accident.

When a powerful storm developed later that same day, it proved to be fortuitous that she had been too sick to go camping with her friends.

Fractious

Unruly, troublesome, or irritable.

The toddler's fractious behavior gave his father a headache.

Garrulous

Exceedingly talkative (especially about unimportant things).

The teacher observed that the students were quite garrulous in the cafeteria and on the playground, but suddenly shy and quiet when asked to discuss a topic during class time.

Grandiloquent

Using pompous or big words (often in an attempt to impress others).

The interviewer's grandiloquent language didn't impress the committee members.

Hackneyed

Seemingly worn out from overuse (often said of a phrase or expression); not seeming fresh and original.

Several of his book reviews criticized his writing for being hackneyed due to his overuse of cliches and common expressions.

Harangue

A loud and lengthy verbal attack.

For a full hour, the superintendent continued his harangue on the workers' insolent behavior.

Hypothesis

An unproven theory made to explain available data or facts (serving as the basis for continued study, testing, or investigation).

The students were asked to write a hypothesis regarding the prospects for terraforming Mars.

Ignominious

Humiliating or degrading (often publicly).

The basketball team was expected to win the game easily; instead, the team suffered an ignominious defeat.

Imperious

Domineering and arrogant.

At first she was excited to work on a group project with the smartest student in the class, but she soon tired of his imperious attitude.

Impervious

Incapable of being penetrated (said of an object) or incapable of being affected (said of a person).

Just a week ago he had loved her so very much, yet now he seemed impervious to the tears streaking down her face.

Impinge

Make an impression or have an effect (usually, in a negative sense).

When the city suggested installing a camera on their street, the homeowners felt that it would impinge on their privacy.

Impudent

Boldly rude or disrespectful.

The teacher sent the student to the principal's office for his impudent behavior.

Impute

Attribute a cause to someone else (usually, of an undesirable outcome).

The teacher imputed the low test scores of her students to a lack of parental support.

Inconsequential

Trivial or unimportant.

He didn't mention the telephone call earlier because it had seemed inconsequential at the time, but now the guard believes that the telephone call was intentionally made to distract him from his duties.

Integrity

Being honest and following a strong code of morals.

Nobody questioned the integrity of the Pope.

Intrepid

Bold and fearless.

The intrepid mountain climbers didn't turn back when the storm approached.

Jubilation

Joy and celebration.

The crowd expressed their jubilation after the home-town baseball team's star player hit a game-winning homerun.

Juxtaposition

Placing two things side-by-side or close together in order to compare the differences between them.

The juxtaposition of the two bicycles shows that the red bicycle has larger wheels and a higher seat than the blue bicycle.

Languid

Weak or sluggish.

Many tourists feel languid in this hot and humid environment.

Latent

Present, but hidden or undeveloped.

The crime scene was dusted for latent fingerprints.

Malevolent

Malicious; wishing for harm to fall upon on others.

The czar was known as a malevolent ruler.

Modicum

Small amount.

Learning to play catch only takes a modicum of training.

Morass

Swamp, bog, or marsh (often used figuratively regarding a complicated or troublesome situation).

Many businesses found themselves in a financial morass when the recession struck.

Writing Practice Workbook

Mundane

Ordinary or commonplace.

Working on the assembly line made her feel like a robot working on a mundane job.

Munificent

Lavish or generous.

A highly successful alumni presented a munificent gift to the university.

Writing Practice Workbook

Nadir

The lowest point.

The automobile manufacturer's nadir was reached after the CEO was caught in a scandal.

Nonchalant

Acting calm, casual, and without worry.

Although the surgeon appeared nonchalant while performing a life or death operation, he displayed his emotions when the surgery was completed.

Writing Practice Workbook

Oblique

Indirect, slanting; not straight to the point.

She spent hours puzzling over the poet's frequent use of oblique metaphors.

Obtuse

Slow to understand something.

Regarding a student who asked simple questions throughout the lecture, the professor wondered if that student was really so obtuse or if he just wasn't paying much attention.

Odious

Very offensive, disgusting, unpleasant, or hateful.

Out of habit, he reached for his cup, not realizing that the chocolate milk had been sitting in the heat for hours. Although he only took a quick sip, it left an odious taste in his mouth.

Officious

Intrusively providing unwanted services or offering unwanted advice (often acting as if they have more importance or authority than that which is perceived by others).

The officious bureaucrat delayed the family reunion for hours over rather trivial matters.

Perfidious

Disloyal, deceitful, treacherous, or traitorous.

In that country, the government has a reputation for being quite perfidious.

Portent

Omen (often for an unfortunate event).

He regarded the black cat crossing the road as a portent of something unpleasant to come.

Pretentious

Attempting to impress others by pretending to be more important or knowledgeable than one really is.

Her friend seemed pretentious, often bragging about his so-called royal relatives.

Primeval

Ancient (relating to the earliest time in history).

Hiking through the primeval forest at night proved to be a very frightening experience.

Prosaic

Ordinary, dull, or lacking imagination.

On the surface, he appeared to live a very prosaic lifestyle, but once she got to know him better, she discovered that he also had a spontaneous side that could be quite exciting.

Puerile

Silly in a childish way.

His puerile behavior often embarrassed his coworkers.

Punctilious

Highly attentive to detail.

My mother is so punctilious about arranging her clothes that even the hangers are color-coded.

Quagmire

A difficult, complex, dangerous, or awkward situation.

Using her rent money to purchase a new outfit and shoes left her in a financial quagmire.

Querulous

Complaining (especially, finding fault).

The querulous couple sitting across from us at dinner seemed to find something wrong with every little detail; their complaints never ceased.

Rancor

Bitter resentment (often deep-seated).

It was surprising to see how much rancor she harbored over her neighbor's barking dog.

Reprove

Express disapproval; scold.

She knew that her parents would reprove of her tattoo and purple hair.

Resilient

Quick to recover or bounce back.

Despite the destruction from the tornado, the community was resilient and quickly returned to their usual good-natured ways.

Reverence

Deep respect and awe.

The Pope is always treated with great reverence.

Sagacity

Good judgment and the ability to make good decisions.

She blamed their financial problems on her husband's lack of sagacity.

Salient

Significant; standing out.

The lecture only covered the salient features of the theory; it didn't get into any of the intricacies with which most students struggle.

Solicitous

Showing care and concern (often anxiously).

The solicitous parents waited all night for their daughter to return home safely with her date.

Spurious

False or fake.

The evidence proved that the suspect had given a spurious alibi.

Substantiate

Provide supporting evidence; prove something.

A reporter must substantiate a story before it is published.

Superficial

Shallow; on the surface; not profound.

The applicant wasn't a good candidate for the position because he had only a superficial knowledge of the job duties.

Superfluous

Extra; more than is needed.

The business had to cut all superfluous expenses in order to avoid filing for bankruptcy.

Taciturn

Seldom talking.

When I was young, I was a taciturn child who almost never voiced my thoughts.

Tenacious

Persistent; determined; stubborn.

She was a tenacious competitor: She would try her hardest until the match was over.

Transient

Lasting for a brief time.

Unfortunately, as much as they enjoyed each other's company, it would only be a transient romance, lasting just for the summer.

Umbrage

Resentment, offense, or annoyance (often regarding a perceived social snub or insult).

Many readers took umbrage to the comments made in an article about common parenting mistakes.

Venerable

Worthy of respect or honor due to age, position, or character.

Many women in the village sought the advice of his venerable grandmother.

Veracity

Truthfulness or accuracy.

The story was so incredible that it was only natural to question its veracity.

Vindicated

Cleared from blame, accusation, suspicion, or criticism.

The evidence vindicated the woman of the crime that she had been accused of.

Wanton

Deliberate, excessive, and without reason (usually regarding cruel actions).

The mayor vowed to put an end to the city's wanton vandalism.

Winsome

Attractive or charming in an innocent way.

The actress never seems to age, and her winsome looks get her many starring roles.

Zenith

Highest point.

He reached the zenith of his career when he was named president of the company.

The Write-N-Learn Series

Douglas Grey

Writing helps with memory

Made in the USA
Columbia, SC
09 June 2019